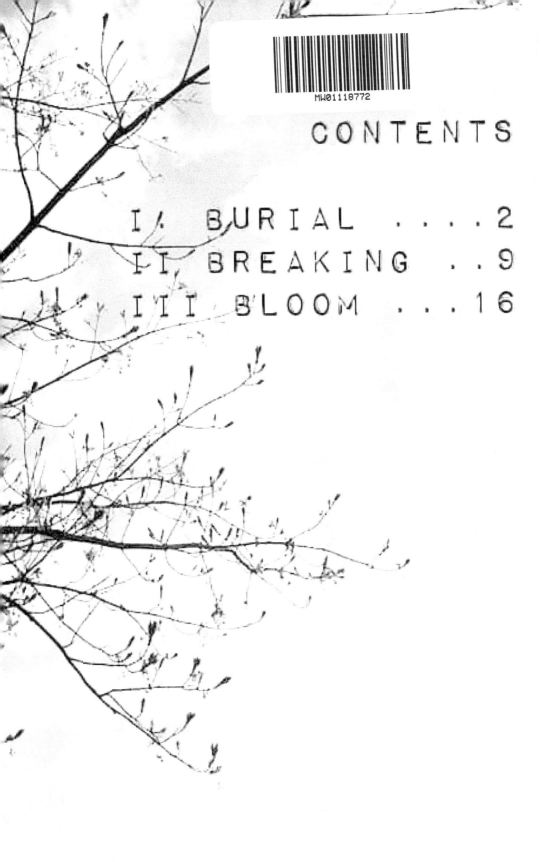

CONTENTS

CHAPTER I

'BURIAL'

SHHHHH SHHHHH SHHHHH.
THE QUIETING OF
A STORM WITHIN
THE WHITE NOISE OF
A SOUL GOING MAD
THE SOUND OF SECRETS
LEAKING OUT LIKE AIR
STORIES OF SHAME AND GUILT
OF PAIN AND STUPIDITY
ESCAPING FROM THE BALLOON
OF MY MIND.

QUICK!
SOMEONE PLUG THE HOLE
SO I'M NOT LAID BARE
BEFORE YOU
BOARD THE WINDOWS
COVER YOUR EARS
BUSY YOUR LIVES

PAY NO ATTENTION
TO THE WOMAN BEHIND
THE CURTAIN...
SHHHHHHHHHH

```
I AM 37
I AM 3
I AM OUTSIDE YOUR CIRCLE
WATCHING YOU PLAY GAMES
(YOUR FUN TASTES LIKE RAGE)


- UNINVITED
```

THE INVISIBLE CHILD
PLAYS WITH DOLLS IN HER ROOM

(HERE IS THE CHURCH)

AND PLAYS
HIDE AND GO SEEK IN HER CLOSET

(HERE IS THE STEEPLE)

IS THIS HER SANCTUARY?
OR
IS SHE THE SACRIFICE...

(OPEN THE DOORS AND
SEE ALL THE PEOPLE)

- INVISIBLE CHILD

"I DON'T REMEMBER"
HAD BEEN HER REFRAIN
FOR SO MANY FRAGMENTED YEARS
THAT HER 37 SEEMED MORE LIKE
A FEW FUZZY MEMORIES
NOT EVEN SURE SHE EXISTED
IN THE FIRST PLACE
STRINGING LINE BETWEEN THE CUPS
PERHAPS SHE IS A LOST DREAM

(MAKEUPMAKEUPMAKEUP)

THE LITTLE GIRL
THAT WAS ME BEFORE I DIED
WAS NOT CREATED
IN GAMES TO HIDE
AND YET SHE COULD
SHOVE HERSELF INTO
ALMOST ANY CORNER
AND DISAPPEAR FOR HOURS
OR WEEKS
OR YEARS

BUT THERE WAS NEVER
A SEARCH PARTY SENT
NO RESCUE UPON
WHITENED STEED
SEEKING ISN'T A PRIORITY
WHEN YOU'RE THE REASON
FOR THE DISAPPEARING

GO ABOUT YOUR BUSINESS
NOTHING
TO
SEE

HERE

LIES

ME

There is always so much to say.
Words as thoughts tumbling across the desert of my
mind. I've written a novel already tonight in my
head.... and yet it all seems so inconsequential after
the thought is gone.

So many burnt words. So much smoke. As if what was
momentarily of great importance just billows away in
the end.

Meaningless. A chasing after the wind.

Are these thoughts even worth penning? Most can't
comprehend a life of pain and those that are familiar
with this sort of existance are only cozy with their
personal earthquakes, not mine.
Sigh.
Let the muck settle into the cracks.
*Silence, you maddening itch, just below the surface
of my mind.*

I hate seeing the end from the beginning. Even if it
is one of my greatest superpowers. Razor sharp
intuition about the impending disaster and the
cataclysmic damage it will rend.   You see, every
moment from the beginning until that God forsaken end
is spent in an enveloping tension, white knuckle fear,
waiting for the moment of impact. There is a veritable
timeline laid prostrate before me of "cause" and its
inevitable "effect". Set at the destruction of my
world.

"How incredible your insight!" you say.
No. How hopeless a curse.

Because the more desperately or wildly I scramble to
alter the ending, the more damage is done by these
graspings.

Pain deferred still ends in pain.

And what could I do about the problem of pain? Ignore,
excuse, cover-up, make light of, scream at, laugh at,
weep over, or build walls around? Drink it away, fuck
it away, smoke it away, bleed it away?! Eat it, throw
it up, stay busy, stay alive, die a thousand deaths
that no one else would notice. Smile. Forever smile
and call all of this "just fine." Except I no longer
have such luxuries. I have taken the "fine" away. I
threw my last "fine" off the cliff and watched it
drown in the bay below.

All I have is this gaping, raw, festering wound for all the world to see. See? See me?! The freak with her emotions on her skin. The zipper on the outside so you can open me again and again. Dig around in the rubble, play with my sick, and zip me back up.

Pain deferred still ends in pain. Just below the surface of my mind.

- March Maddening.

CHAPTER II

'BREAKING'

She sucks air in like

She was taking a big drag off a pall mall cigarette

And holds the oxygen in her lungs for too long

So she can taste the burning of yesterday

Too long

Since her lungs were filled with

Smoke and mirrors

Angry tears

C a s c a d e

Waterfalls and timid brooks

Upon her cheeks as she exhales loudly

Like an alarm for attention

Like a   LOOKATMEYOUDUMBFUCKER!!!!

* sigh *

He lives too far inside himself and those

Walls he built are soundproof

Waterproof

Her.Proof.

And so they sit like foreigners in a refugee camp

Haunted by the past

Hunted by the present...

Prove to her you aren't You!

Aren't the poison in her veins

The stains of memories beneath her skin

* sigh *

She sucks air in like she was taking a hit from a

Bullet

t r a i n

YOU ARE WHAT YOU EAT
AND I'VE SWALLOWED YOUR PAIN
ALL YOUR RAGE, YEARS OF BLAME
STUFFED BETWEEN PIECES OF MEAT
SMEARED WITH TWICE EMPTY PROMISES
CUT INTO MORSELS, JUST SO
SHOVED AS FISTS DOWN MY THROAT
SHOVED AS HATE DOWN MY SOUL

BUT   I CAN'T DIGEST YOU
AND NO MATTER HOW MANY TIMES
I PUT MY FINGERS DOWN MY THROAT
I CAN'T EXPEL YOU

BECAUSE 17 YEARS FEELS LIKE AN ANVIL
BETWEEN MY RIBS
AND YOUR SILENCES
AND ANGRY GLARES
TASTE OF VINEGAR AND TEARS

SEE?!?!
I'M LOOKING MORE AND MORE LIKE REGRET WITH EACH MEAL
SEE?!?!
i'M LOOKING LESS AND LESS LIKE ALIVE WITH EACH YEAR

- Last Supper

11

AND HOW SHOULD I LAUGH
LOUD, EXTRAVAGANT, PROUD?
    YOU STRIPPED AWAY MY FANTASY
    HUNG MY HOPE ON SOME CLOUD
WHILE I CLIMB UP YOUR LIMBS
WHILE YOUR SPINE GIVES AWAY
    I AM TREMBLING BLUE
    FATALISTIC PARADE
HOW THOSE LIPS DRIBBLE TALES
ONLY YOUR EARS RECEIVE
    DOVES DEVOURED BY SHARKS
    CRUSHED BETWEEN LOVERS TEETH
CHAIN ME TO ANOTHER ROCK
THROW MY HEART TO THE DEEP
    I'LL TAKE MY FANCY WITH SIRENS
    TO HOLD AND TO KEEP

- ANOTHER SIREN SONG

MAKING LOVE TO YOU FEELS LIKE
SIPHONING YOUR STRESS
     YOUR BREATH TASTES OF SECOND THOUGHTS
     SWIRLING AROUND IN MY HEAD
        YOU'RE JUDAS AFTER HIS KISS

        YOU'RE LUCIFER BEFORE HIS FALL
     MY BELOVED IS A SHADOW
     I USED TO TRACE ON THE WALL
STOP EMPTYING YOUR DARKNESS INTO ME
I AM NOT YOUR WORRY DOLL

I AM NOT
YOUR GHOST
I AM NOT
YOUR GHOST
I AM NOT WANDERING
GROPING
FOR FLESH
AND BONE
OR TO BE KNOWN
I AM MY OWN
MY. OWN.

- DISAPPEARING ACT

I've been more afraid of the light

Than of echoes in the darkness

My arms accustomed to wrapping around my fragile frame

My feet accustomed to

Long walks in blackened silence

My ears stuffed with the screams of all my

"NO!!!!'s"

Eyes clenched like fists inside my head

Straightening each picture

Hung as denial on the walls

Haunting memories familiar in that homey kind of way

.Sick.

When freedom feels perilous

And unwrapping your truth

Tastes like so much vomit in your mouth

And those "NO's are trusted friends

That snake their way under your skin

Making love to your bones

Seductively stripping your insides bare.

Sick.

A lifetime of tears that should never have been

Became the lake in which I swim

Watching sunsets linger

Washing shades of grey upon my shore

No!

I've been treading sorrows

Drowning in my existance

For the thousandth night in a row

Sick.

That hope perches as dread upon my stomach

And death hums love songs in my head

CHAPTER III
'BLOOM'

It was heavy and dark

Unbreathing

A lifetime of holding my lungs Hostage

Fear and shame sucking oxygen   away

Darkness my companion and fear my friend

Burried with you

My Lover

My Devil

My Hope

My Hurt

Slowly dying

~

Slowly breaking

Split open   Emerging

Feeling His light upon my skin

Truth gripping me tightly

Pulling me skyward

Through the pain. Through the memories

Eyes opening

The weight of a lifetime spent d i r t y

Falling away in His presence

Limbs stretching skyward over soil

My breath

My life

My sacrifice

My freedom

Alive

- seeds

Before I was born
You set out to destroy me
And you've used every weapon in your arsenal
To end me
I've felt your cold breath upon my skin
Like a familiar friend
Your fingers gripping my heart
Squeezing my life
Until it pours blood and tears upon your feet
Your hollow pit consuming my spirit
The lies, (so many lies)
swimming circles in my mind
Shame undercurrent   Becoming my name

^

Identity, Insanity.
Abuse after abuse
Betrayal upon betrayal
Loss after loss after loss.
Trust shattered
Hope ripped from my palms
Fear burned in lines upon my arms
Fear swallowed in pints, in pills
Breathed as smoke & mirrors into my soul
Fear screamed into my being
from the hands that were to hold me
Till death do us part
Was almost reality
Too many times to count
WHY AM I STILL HERE?

I'M STILL HERE.

still.   here.

My body is broken   but not for you.

My arms, empty and open   but not for you.

My story no longer unspoken

Not locked inside this prison

Not choked. Silently screaming for relief

Mixing Word   as poetry

          As power   as Song

So, you can have these ashes

I know to whom I belong.

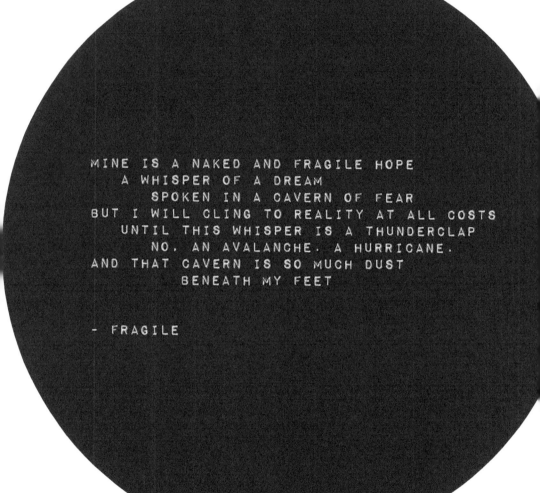

MINE IS A NAKED AND FRAGILE HOPE
   A WHISPER OF A DREAM
      SPOKEN IN A CAVERN OF FEAR
BUT I WILL CLING TO REALITY AT ALL COSTS
   UNTIL THIS WHISPER IS A THUNDERCLAP
      NO. AN AVALANCHE. A HURRICANE.
AND THAT CAVERN IS SO MUCH DUST
      BENEATH MY FEET

- FRAGILE

ON A DAY PREGNANT WITH TEARS
THE KIND OF SPILLING OVER
THAT COMES FROM THE SADDENING
OF 17 YEARS
THE KIND OF MOURNING SONG
THAT LEAVES YOU PUDDLED ON THE
LIVINGROOM FLOOR
HORSE VOICED AND HELPLESS
YES. ON DAYS SUCH AS THESE
THE VERY FABRIC OF HEAVEN
CAN STILL REND
AND LAUGHTER CAN FALL
SPLASHING SWEETNESS UPON YOUR FACE
CREASING THOSE LINES BESIDE YOUR LIPS
IN A FUNNY UPTURNED WAY THAT FEELS
'STRANGE'
BECAUSE IT'S BEEN SO MANY LONG DAYS
'STRANGE'
THAT THE SOUND OF JOY
SHOULD QUICKEN YOUR HEART
WITH BOTH FEAR AND MYSTERIOUS GLEE

OH RAPTUROUS GRIEF
BEWILDER ME

- STRANGE

I wish words were enough

Heavier. Thick.

Dissolving on your tongue

To taste my freedom

Quickening your heartbeat

Alive at last

The breath of my new life

Warm upon your cheek.

I shed my old skin

Not for you

For me   (FOR ME)

Because I hated her fear

Her stink   Her lies

Her excuses   Her shame

The ways she made herself smaller

I was not made to see her reflection in my mirror

That stranger possessing all of my rage

So I killed her. I died.

I buried the lies.

Set fire to that life

To resurrect me.

- Resurrection Song

And now rubble has settled

Ashes and dust

Annihilation of all that corrupted

The pureness of love

That scared little girl

With her scars and her shame

Was burned alive at the stake

By a Holy flame

The hounds of her hell

The demons she once entertained

Are no longer invited to

Come play their games

That girl you once knew

Doesn't live here anymore

And the one you will meet

Climbs higher than before

You can't touch her heat

Her brave will blister your skin

The light of her truth

Makes the darkness cringe

She shatters her grave

Sets her wings to the skies

No earth holds her captive

With the flames she shall rise.

I HELD MY OWN HEAD
IN MY OWN HANDS
STARED AT MY OWN EYES
IN THE BATHROOM MIRROR

I SPOKE EVERY POEM
& SANG EVERY LOVE SONG
TO THE TUNE ONLY MY
EARS COULD HEAR

I PENETRATED MY WALLS
BROKE DOWN EACH DEFENSE
& SPILLED HOPE INTO
EVERY WOUND

AND AT THE END OF
MY SELF LOVE MAKING
I ROCKED MY BODY TO
SLEEP WITH THIS TUNE

I AM ENOUGH.
I AM ENOUGH.
I AM ENOUGH.

CPSIA information can be obtained
at www.ICGtesting.com
Printed in the USA
BVHW042211271118
534078BV00011B/9/P